# Leading With Liberty

## How to Lead in a Multicultural World

Sharath K Bhaskaran

# DEDICATION

To every individual who has dared to lead with principle over comfort, with purpose over pride, and with liberty as their compass.
To the quiet builders, brave reformers, and bold visionaries—from Gandhi's peaceful defiance to Douglass's uncompromising voice, from Yunus's economic empathy to Mandela's forgiving strength, from Jefferson's ideals to Churchill's resolve, from Toyoda's thoughtful systems to Jobs's restless innovation.
And to all those across cultures and continents who continue to lead not by force, but by fostering freedom—this book is for you.
Lead freely. Live fully.

# LEADING WITH LIBERTY

## HOW TO LEAD IN A MUTICULTURAL WORLD

# SHARATH K BHASKARAN

# CONTENTS

# ACKNOWLEDGMENTS

This book stands on the shoulders of visionaries who led with courage, conviction, and a deep respect for human liberty. To Mahatma Gandhi, who showed the power of nonviolent resistance; to Frederick Douglass, who spoke truth to power in the fight for dignity; and to Muhammad Yunus, who reimagined economic freedom from the ground up. We honor Bill Gates for leveraging innovation to solve global problems, and Steve Jobs for proving that bold vision can shape the future. To Thomas Jefferson and James Madison, whose foundational belief in liberty lit the path for democratic governance; and to Winston Churchill, who reminded the world that liberty must be defended even when it is costly. We are inspired by Nelson Mandela, who turned forgiveness into a force for national rebirth, and Kiichiro Toyoda, who quietly built systems of empowerment through continuous improvement.

We also acknowledge Ray Dalio, whose insights on radical transparency and thoughtful disagreement have reshaped our understanding of leadership and decision-making. His approach to organizational culture and meritocracy has proven that successful leadership is grounded in openness and accountability. To Jordan B. Peterson, whose exploration of individual responsibility and the role of cultural values in shaping human behavior has deepened our understanding of the complexities of leadership in a multicultural world. His teachings challenge us to confront the chaos of modern life with discipline and meaning, reminding us that leadership begins with the individual and radiates outward. Their legacies remind us that great leadership in a multicultural world begins not with power—but with principle

# 1 LIBERTY AS THE ULTIMATE AIM

Every day, across continents and time zones, people who have never met work together in perfect harmony—without even realizing it. A coder in Bangalore, a coffee farmer in Colombia, a truck driver in Nebraska, and a designer in Nairobi all play roles in creating the phone in your hand, the chair you're sitting on, or the coffee you're sipping while reading this book.

No central planner orchestrated this collaboration. No government committee assigned the roles. It is the silent, elegant coordination of the price system—the most powerful force of peaceful cooperation in the world.

And why do they participate in this symphony of human productivity? Yes, they earn wages. Yes, they build careers. But peel back the layers, and you'll find the deepest drive is not just survival or material comfort. It is the pursuit of liberty—the ability to shape one's own life, to choose one's path, to live uncoerced.

This is not a metaphor. This is economics as freedom in action.

**The Price System: A Universal Language of Cooperation**

Unlike spoken language or cultural rituals, the price system transcends national borders and ethnic divisions. It speaks to everyone equally. Prices are signals, telling people where to direct their effort, where needs exist, where opportunities lie.

A Cambodian garment worker doesn't need to understand the fashion trends in Paris to know her work has value. A Polish programmer doesn't have to share the same religion or politics as a startup founder in Brazil to solve a problem together. They only need to agree on the exchange of value. This shared incentive unites people in ways politics never could.

This is the practical foundation of liberty—mutual benefit without force. It is not merely the absence of coercion; it is the presence of choice, of opportunity, of dignity.

**Leadership in a Multicultural World: Recognizing the Real Goal**

So what does this mean for you, the leader?

It means that everyone you lead—whether they're sitting in the same room or half a world away—shares in this deeper human goal: liberty. Not just political liberty, but personal agency. The ability to choose how to live, what to create, who to become.

Leadership that ignores this misses the point. Leadership that recognizes it becomes a force multiplier.

You are not managing cogs in a machine. You are stewarding individuals who have entrusted part of their freedom to your cause, hoping that it will expand their liberty in return—through growth, income, learning, or meaning.

Whether your team is diverse in language, culture, or continent, they are unified in this: they are all, ultimately, acting to expand their liberty.

**Liberty Is the End of All Action**

This insight—drawn from thinkers like Ludwig von Mises and echoed in the real lives of everyday people—must become a guiding light in your leadership philosophy. If you lead without understanding that liberty is the end goal, you may achieve compliance, but never loyalty. You may extract effort, but not creativity. You may build a team, but never a tribe.

Multicultural leadership is not about managing differences. It's about uncovering the universal. And liberty is the most universal human desire of all.

So, lead with liberty—not as a buzzword, but as your blueprint.

**Case Study: Gandhi's Swaraj Movement — Liberty as the End, Not the Means**

**Case Study: Gandhi's Swaraj Movement — Liberty as the End, Not the Means**

**Background: Colonial Control vs. Individual Liberty**

In the early 20th century, India was under British colonial rule. The British government tightly controlled every facet of Indian life—from economic policy to civil freedoms. Indian salt was taxed. Indian cloth was displaced by British imports. Indian voices were muted in their own land.

Enter **Mohandas Karamchand Gandhi**, a British-educated lawyer who returned to India not with guns or slogans, but with a radical idea: **true freedom (Swaraj) is not just political independence—it is individual self-rule.**

Gandhi's movement was not simply about removing a colonial government. It was about reawakening personal agency, local autonomy, and dignity—especially among the poorest and most oppressed.

**Swaraj: Liberty Through Decentralized Cooperation**

Gandhi's vision of Swaraj meant much more than electing Indian officials. It meant a society in which every village governed itself, every person took ownership of their labour, and **no one needed permission to live with dignity**.

"Real Swaraj will come not by the acquisition of authority by a few," Gandhi wrote,
"but by the acquisition of the capacity by all to resist authority when it is abused."

In your terms: Gandhi was building a system where **no central planner orchestrated the people's cooperation**—they did it themselves, motivated by **shared values and voluntary effort**.

**The Salt March: A Marketplace of Liberty in Motion**

In 1930, Gandhi launched the **Salt March**, a 240-mile trek to the Arabian Sea to make salt—an act made illegal by British law.

This wasn't just protest. It was a **case study in peaceful economic rebellion**. Gandhi didn't need a permit or budget or state decree. He needed only the **voluntary participation** of thousands of ordinary citizens, unified by their desire to act freely.

- A villager joined the march not because they were paid, but because they wanted to reclaim agency.
- A peasant broke the salt law not for political power, but to show they were no longer subjects—they were free individuals.

Just like the coder in Bangalore or the truck driver in Nebraska in your chapter, these citizens didn't need to know one another. They didn't even need to be led in the traditional sense. They only needed a **shared value system that respected individual liberty.**

---

**Leadership Without Coercion: Gandhi as a Liberty-Centered Steward**
Gandhi rejected hierarchy. He called himself a servant, not a ruler. He believed leadership's role was not to command, but to cultivate conditions where people could lead themselves.

- He never demanded blind loyalty; he **invited conscious participation.**
- He encouraged debate, dissent, and moral reflection—even from his closest allies.
- He didn't build systems of enforcement. He built **communities of commitment.**

As you write in *Lead with Liberty,*
"You are not managing cogs in a machine. You are stewarding individuals who have entrusted part of their freedom to your cause…"
Gandhi lived this truth. And that's why his movement endured beyond his lifetime—because it was never *his* movement to begin with. It belonged to the people.

---

**Why This Case Study Matters Today**
In a world of multicultural teams, global collaboration, and decentralized work, Gandhi's model is strikingly modern.

- He led across religious, linguistic, and regional boundaries— without enforcing uniformity.
- He proved that people will unite not under pressure, but under **purpose.**
- He showed that **liberty isn't just a moral right—it's a functional necessity** for sustainable cooperation.

Like the price system, Gandhi's movement was a **marketplace of moral coordination.** No one assigned roles. No one distributed liberty. People acted freely—and in doing so, they made freedom real for others.

---

**Leadership Takeaway: Liberty Scales When You Let It**
Gandhi didn't scale his leadership by force or funding. He scaled it by trusting people to act with **conscience and agency.** His methods didn't rely on compliance. They relied on **belief**—the belief that every human being deserves to shape their life without coercion.
As a modern leader, your job is not to plan every move. It is to create the space for others to move with purpose.
Liberty, Gandhi taught us, isn't the prize at the end of the struggle.
It's the **starting condition** that makes every human endeavour worthwhile.

Leading With Liberty: How to Lead in a Multicultural World

Here are five key lessons and principles from the chapter and Gandhi's case study:

- **Liberty is the Foundation, Not the Reward**
  True leadership begins by honouring individuals' agency—liberty isn't a goal after success, it's the condition that makes success possible.
- **Voluntary Cooperation is More Powerful Than Forced Compliance**
  Real, lasting impact comes when people act from belief and purpose, not pressure or authority.
- **Leaders Are Stewards, Not Controllers**
  Effective leadership creates conditions for others to lead themselves—through trust, transparency, and shared values.
- **Cultural Diversity Doesn't Divide When Liberty Unites**
  People of different backgrounds can collaborate meaningfully when they are free to choose and contribute as equals.
- **Decentralization Empowers and Scales Leadership**
  The most scalable systems are those that rely on local ownership, moral conviction, and freedom—not top-down control.

# 2 FOUNDATIONS OF FREEDOM: VOLUNTARISM IN PRACTICE

When someone chooses to work with you—whether they're dialling in from a beach in Bali, a high-rise in Toronto, or a shelter in a war-torn region—they are not just saying "yes" to a pay check. They are saying "yes" to an idea.

That idea is voluntarism—the principle that every interaction should be rooted in consent, not coercion. In a multicultural team, this principle is not optional. It's foundational.

Each person you lead has voluntarily chosen to ease some of their burdens by exchanging their time, energy, and talent for something they believe will better their life—be it income, purpose, connection, or freedom. That is sacred. That is powerful.

**From Boston to Baghdad: Voluntarism Is Not New**

Let's rewind to a crisp December night in 1773. A group of colonists, fed up with being taxed without representation, climbed aboard British ships and dumped 342 chests of tea into Boston Harbor. The Boston Tea Party wasn't just a protest—it was a declaration of dignity. A line in the sand. A signal that voluntarism would no longer be optional in governance.

That night sparked a revolution. And when the dust settled, America's Founding Fathers sat down not to install a king or to divide up spoils, but to debate how a government could be restrained, how power could be limited, how freedom could be preserved through checks and balances, federalism, and the separation of church and state.

Why? Because they understood a core truth: free people do not exist to serve institutions. Institutions exist to serve free people.

And this, dear leader, is exactly the mindset you must bring to your multicultural workplace.

**Voluntarism Is the Engine of Multicultural Cooperation**

In today's world, your "company" may include a refugee from Syria handling customer service, a home-schooling dad in Oklahoma coding your app, a digital nomad in Lisbon designing your brand, and a fresh grad in Seoul running your social media.

They didn't join you because they were drafted. They chose you. Choose your mission. Chose to bet on your vision.

What you are witnessing is not just diversity—it's decentralized cooperation. It's voluntarism in action. No coercion. Just mutual benefit.

You don't need quotas or sensitivity training to make this work. You need to lead like a founder of a new republic—recognizing that every person under your banner is a sovereign in their own right.

**The New Checks and Balances**

The American Founders embedded a system of checks and balances to ensure no one person or institution could dominate the rest. This wasn't a glitch—it was the feature. Because when power is limited, freedom flourishes.

So ask yourself: In your team, where is the power too concentrated? Where can you decentralize decision-making? Can your designers veto a bad marketing call? Can your junior staff question your strategy? Can your freelancers walk away if they feel unheard?

These are not HR policies. These are constitutional principles.

**The Modern Multicultural Republic**

To lead in a multicultural world is to build a republic of shared purpose. It means:

- **Creating voluntary alliances** based on mutual gain, not forced conformity.
- **Protecting freedom of conscience**—your people should never have to lie about who they are to belong.
- **Practicing subsidiarity**—let decisions be made as close to the source as possible.
- **Fostering pluralism**—not erasing differences but harmonizing them through common cause.

Your team is not a melting pot. It's an orchestra. Everyone brings their instrument. Your job is not to make them identical—it's to make them play in tune.

**Lead Like a Founder, Not a Boss**

The Founding Fathers didn't build a flawless system—but they aimed at liberty, and liberty, imperfect as it is, remains the only system under which genuine multicultural cooperation can endure.

As a leader, you don't need to be perfect either. But you do need to be principled. Start by recognizing that your power flows from consent. That each person who joins your mission is not an employee in the old sense, but a free actor who has chosen, voluntarily, to share in your journey.

So honour that choice. Lead with liberty.

13

14

**A Leadership Case Study:** *Frederick Douglass and the Power of Voluntary Association*

**A Leadership Case Study:** *Frederick Douglass and the Power of Voluntary Association*

16

# Leading With Liberty: How to Lead in a Multicultural World

**A Leadership Case Study:** *Frederick Douglass and the Power of Voluntary Association*

In the mid-19th century, as America grappled with the moral stain of slavery, **Frederick Douglass**, born into bondage and self-liberated through sheer will, became one of the clearest voices for liberty—not only as a political ideal, but as a principle of **voluntary human cooperation.**

After escaping slavery in 1838, Douglass didn't just fight for abolition—he **built institutions**, led publications, and launched a powerful speaking career. But more importantly, he led a movement rooted in *voluntarism*. He didn't coerce people into joining the cause for freedom. He invited them. Through persuasion, reason, and personal narrative, he united abolitionists, former slaves, religious leaders, feminists, and working-class allies across national and ideological lines.

### The Liberty-Fuelled Team Behind *The North Star*

In 1847, Douglass founded an anti-slavery newspaper, *The North Star*, with the motto: **"Right is of no sex, Truth is of no color, God is the Father of us all, and we are all brethren."**

But this wasn't just a media project—it was a **voluntary multicultural coalition**. His co-editor, **Martin Delany**, was a free-born Black doctor and intellectual. The paper was funded not by any central institution, but by voluntary contributions from supporters across the U.S. and Britain—people who believed in the mission of emancipation.

The contributors and team members included Irish immigrants, white Quaker abolitionists, and free Black intellectuals—each bringing different skills, backgrounds, and ideas. What united them wasn't similarity. It was **shared purpose**—the belief that all human beings are entitled to agency over their own lives.

They weren't *told* to serve. They *chose* to serve. And Douglass made it clear that he **welcomed ideas, dissent, and diversity**, as long as the shared goal remained freedom.

### Voluntarism as an Ethical Blueprint

Douglass understood that moral clarity alone wasn't enough. People had to come to the cause freely. That's why he refused to align himself fully with political parties, resisted dogma, and emphasized **principled pluralism**. His leadership respected the agency of others—even those who disagreed on methods—as long as they respected liberty as the end.

He also had an instinctive sense of **subsidiarity**. He believed in change from the ground up—local action, personal responsibility, and the voice of the community. He practiced what many leaders in multicultural organizations today strive for: **decentralized moral**

**leadership**.

This was voluntarism at its finest—not abstract, but embodied in the everyday work of organizing, writing, advocating, and listening.

---

### Why Douglass Matters for Today's Leaders

Modern multicultural teams face the same challenge Douglass faced: how to bring together people from different walks of life without forcing them to conform. How to lead by principle, not by policy. How to build cooperation on **shared values**, not shallow consensus.

Douglass shows us that the foundation of voluntary association is **dignity**—respecting each individual's freedom to say *yes*, and their equal freedom to walk away. When people know they are not prisoners of your mission but partners in it, they will give not only their labor—but their creativity, honesty, and courage.

**That's the real power of voluntary leadership**. It doesn't extract. It attracts. It doesn't control. It compels by clarity of purpose.

So, if you're building a company, a school, a nonprofit, or a remote team with people across borders, **lead like Douglass**. Make your mission clear. Invite others to join—not because they have to, but because they want to.

Because in every era and every culture, liberty begins where **voluntarism is respected**—and only leaders who understand that can truly unite diverse minds in common cause.

Here are five key lessons and principles from the chapter and Frederick Douglass's leadership case study:

- **Voluntarism is the Heart of True Leadership**
  People must be free to choose their involvement—this freedom builds trust, creativity, and authentic commitment.
- **Shared Purpose, Not Forced Unity, Builds Diverse Teams**
  Multicultural cooperation thrives when people rally around a mission, not when they're asked to fit a mold.
- **Decentralized Leadership Respects Local Wisdom**
  Let those closest to the issue lead; subsidiarity empowers individuals and strengthens collective impact.
- **Dignity is the Basis of All Voluntary Association**
  Respect for each person's agency—especially their right to say "no"—creates a culture of mutual respect and principled engagement.
- **Leadership by Invitation, Not Imposition, Endures**
  Like Douglass, effective leaders persuade with moral clarity, not control, attracting allies instead of managing subjects.

# 3 EMPOWERMENT THROUGH VALUE CREATION

In the fog of modern leadership lingo, one word still cuts through clearly: *value.*

Your team, your customers, your users—they all want the same thing: to matter. And in the realm of multicultural leadership, where language, religion, culture, and even time zones may differ, shared *value creation* becomes the great equalizer. It gives meaning to the work and coherence to the mission.

But here's the catch: value isn't created by command. It's created by clarity.

**Communicate the Real-World Problem**

Before you can lead a team to solve a problem, you must name it. Not in abstract corporate language. Not in slide decks or slogans. But in plain, human terms:

- If you're building financial tools: "We're helping people escape debt traps and own their future."
- If you're in public health: "We're reducing suffering and increasing life expectancy, one decision at a time."
- If you're building software: "We're helping people do more with less stress, and get their time back."

Without this clarity, your multicultural team might work hard but spin in circles. They won't know *what* trade-offs are worth making—or *why* they're even working late. But once they understand the "why," they begin to lead themselves.

**Trade-Offs: The Currency of Progress**

Every mission has its price. That price might be:

- **Tight deadlines** to reach a launch that serves people on time.
- **Creative constraints** to keep the product intuitive for users from vastly different backgrounds.
- **Constant iteration** to stay relevant to a community whose needs are evolving.

As a leader, your job is to *frame those trade-offs* not as burdens, but as investments—into something worthy. A better world. A more useful tool. A public that's empowered.

This works across all cultures. Why? Because it speaks to a universal law: we are willing to give up ease, comfort, even sleep—for something that *matters.*

**Incentives: Designed for Purpose, Not Politics**

Now, how do you align incentives—especially if you're not a startup with stock options, but a public institution or a non-profit?

Simple. You design for *reciprocity.*

If you're in the private sector, your goal is to ensure that the product or service is so good, people are not just willing, but *happy* to pay for it.

But if you're in the public sector, where direct payment may not exist, you must design *proxy systems* that mimic market feedback:

- **Vouchers** for parents that can be spent at any accredited school—public, private, or co-op—give them agency and signal what systems are actually working.
- **Service-level feedback** from citizens that tie public funding to public satisfaction ensures that bureaucracies serve, rather than stagnate.
- **Merit-based bonuses** for public workers tied to actual public outcomes—not just hours clocked or boxes checked—align effort with real-world results.

Whether you're leading a startup or a city council, the principle holds: *value must be visible, incentives must be aligned, and the mission must be felt.*

### Empowerment Is Not a Pep Talk—It's a System

You don't empower people by saying, "You're empowered." You empower them by:

- Giving them clear goals.
- Letting them see how their work moves the mission forward.
- Rewarding them not for presence, but for *progress*.

And you do all this *regardless* of where they come from. Because when someone from São Paulo and someone from Sarajevo can both say, "We're solving the same problem, together," you've cracked the code of multicultural leadership.

### Serve the Mission, Not the Org Chart

When everyone is working toward value—real, felt, measurable value—they stop obsessing over titles, turf wars, and job descriptions. They start obsessing over outcomes. Over impact. Over people.

And that's when the magic happens.

In a world divided by borders, politics, and algorithms, value creation is one of the last honest languages we all still speak.

So speak it fluently. Lead with it proudly.

23

**A Leadership Case Study:** *Muhammad Yunus and the Rise of Microcredit*

26

**A Leadership Case Study: *Muhammad Yunus and the Rise of Microcredit***

In the 1970s, Bangladesh was recovering from war and famine. Its people—especially women in rural areas—lived in a cycle of poverty where even a few dollars in capital were impossible to obtain. Traditional banks refused to lend to the poor. Bureaucracies were bloated and disconnected. Aid organizations focused on handouts, not solutions.

Into this void stepped **Muhammad Yunus**, an economics professor who realized that the problem wasn't a lack of work ethic or ideas. The problem was systemic: people lacked access to capital. And without that, they couldn't create value—no matter how talented, driven, or entrepreneurial they were.

**Step 1: Naming the Real Problem in Human Terms**

Yunus didn't talk about GDP or economic development. He talked about people. Specifically, a group of 42 women in a village near Chittagong who were making bamboo stools but trapped in debt to local moneylenders. They needed about **$27 USD**—total—to break free and buy raw materials on fair terms.

So he gave it to them. Out of his own pocket.

And when they repaid him, on time and with dignity, a new idea was born—not just an economic idea, but a leadership philosophy:

*"Credit is a human right."*

He framed the problem in a way his multicultural team—and the world—could understand: people weren't poor because they were lazy or unskilled. They were poor because they were excluded from the system. Value creation was impossible without inclusion.

**Step 2: Making the Trade-Offs Visible**

As Grameen Bank evolved from this one act of generosity into a global force, Yunus faced resistance at every level—from regulators, traditional economists, and even global aid organizations. But he kept the mission laser-clear:

- **Trade-off 1:** Risk small amounts of money to help many people escape generational poverty.
- **Trade-off 2:** Trust in social collateral (peer groups) over traditional credit scores.
- **Trade-off 3:** Operate with tiny margins in exchange for massive social value.

He didn't sugarcoat the costs. He reframed them as investments in human potential. And his team—many of whom came from vastly different backgrounds—aligned around the outcome, not the obstacles.

**Step 3: Designing Incentives for Purpose, Not Politics**

Grameen Bank's model was revolutionary because it built **market-like feedback into a public good.**

- Loans went to **women**, who statistically were more likely to reinvest in their families and communities.
- Borrowers joined **self-governing groups**, creating peer accountability and mentoring.
- The bank charged **interest**, but only enough to sustain operations—not to enrich shareholders.
- The focus was always on **value creation**—microloans were used to buy cows, plant crops, start sewing businesses, or run food stalls.

People didn't just take money—they built things. And because they had ownership, they repaid at rates higher than traditional borrowers in developed countries.

In public sector terms, this is a *voucher system for economic agency*. It gave people the power to direct their future and signaled what models worked by what people chose.

**Step 4: Systemic Empowerment—Not Pep Talks**

Yunus didn't stand on stages and shout "You're empowered!" Instead:

- He built a **structure that proved trust** in the people it served.
- He created **systems that measured progress**, not just paperwork.
- He staffed his team with **local field officers** who understood cultural nuance and spoke the language of the people—not donors.

The result? Millions of people lifted out of poverty. Entire villages transformed. A global movement that led to **Yunus winning the Nobel Peace Prize in 2006**, not for charity—but for showing the world that **empowerment through value creation** wasn't a theory. It was a replicable system.

---

**Why This Case Study Matters to Today's Leaders**

Whether you're building a startup or leading a public institution, Yunus' story shows that value creation only works when:

- The **problem is human**, not corporate.
- The **trade-offs are respected**, not hidden.
- The **incentives are honest**, not political.
- And the **system empowers**, rather than performs empowerment.

If you want your multicultural team to care, connect, and create— **don't give them slogans. Give them ownership.** Let them see who they're helping, how their work matters, and how their success is tied to real-world impact.

Because no matter where your team is from, **value creation is a common language**. And the leaders who speak it fluently unlock not just output—but meaning, motivation, and momentum.

Here are five key lessons and principles from the chapter and Muhammad Yunus's leadership case study:

- **Value Creation Begins with Human Clarity**
  Define the real-world problem in plain language so every team member understands who they're helping and why it matters.
- **Empowerment Requires Ownership, Not Overhead**
  True empowerment comes from systems that let people see, feel, and direct their own impact—not just motivational slogans.
- **Visible Trade-Offs Inspire Trust and Commitment**
  Frame sacrifices as purposeful investments toward meaningful outcomes, not arbitrary demands.
- **Design Incentives That Reflect Purpose, Not Politics**
  Align rewards with real-world outcomes and make success measurable through human impact, not hierarchy.
- **Inclusion Is the Foundation of Value Creation**
  If people are excluded from systems, they can't contribute or thrive—empowerment begins by giving everyone a seat at the table.

# 4 STRATEGIC LISTENING — LEADING WITH TIMING AND EMPATHY

If liberty is the foundation of leadership, **listening** is its heartbeat. We often hear that leaders need to "communicate clearly," and yes, that's important. But here's the truth: most conflicts, disengagements, and even breakdowns in multicultural teams don't happen because someone said the wrong thing.

They happen because someone felt unheard.

**Listening Is Not Hearing**

To lead with liberty, you must understand that listening is not a passive skill. It's an **active strategy**—one that builds trust, reveals insights, diffuses tension, and invites innovation.

This is especially crucial in multicultural environments, where cultural norms around speaking up, giving feedback, or challenging authority vary wildly.

In some cultures, silence means agreement. In others, it means disagreement. In some, questioning leadership is a sign of respect. In others, it's seen as betrayal. As a leader, your job is to decode these silences—and respond strategically.

**The Leadership Edge: Know When to Speak, When to Stay Silent**

Listening is a form of timing. And timing, in leadership, is everything.

- **Speak too soon**, and you might smother an idea before it's formed.
- **Speak too late**, and people will assume you're out of touch.
- **Stay quiet forever**, and your silence becomes complicity.

Empathy is the compass. Timing is the map.

**Listen Before the Boiling Point**

Most leaders only start listening when the situation is already on fire—when morale drops, when projects stall, when someone finally explodes in a meeting.

But strategic listening means you're **tuning in before the crisis**. Create structured, predictable spaces for people to speak:

- **Regular one-on-ones** that aren't just about metrics, but about meaning.
- **Anonymous feedback tools** that allow voices who fear judgment to still be heard.
- **"Temperature checks"** in meetings where people rate how aligned or confused, they feel.
- **"Elephant Spotting" sessions** where the unspoken becomes speak-able.

In a multicultural team, assume there *is* something people are not saying. Your job is to make it sayable.

**Name the Elephant First**

There's always an elephant in the room.

Maybe it's a cultural misstep no one wants to bring up. Maybe it's a tension between departments. Maybe it's a failed launch, an unpopular decision, or just an air of quiet discontent.

And here's where leadership comes in: **be the first to speak**.

When people are afraid to say the thing that needs saying, **you must be the one who says it first.** Not to accuse. Not to control. But to liberate the room.

Try:

- "I get the feeling we're avoiding something—can we speak openly for a moment?"
- "I'm worried I may have made a call that didn't land well. Let's unpack it."
- "There's a tension here, and I'd rather we address it directly than let it fester."

By naming the unspeakable, you de-weaponize it. You set the tone. You build psychological safety—and that's the bedrock of multicultural trust.

## Listening as Empowerment

To listen is to empower. And here's why:

When someone feels heard, they stop defending. They start building. They stop hiding. They start contributing.

In a remote team, this might mean making time zones and accents feel like assets, not obstacles. In an in-person team, it might mean rotating who leads meetings or who drafts proposals, to balance dominant voices.

Empowerment through listening isn't a feel-good tactic. It's an operational advantage. Because the people closest to the problem are usually the ones closest to the solution—if you make space for their voice.

## Silence Is Data

Here's a hard truth: when your team goes silent, they're still communicating. Just not with words.

They're telling you:

- "I don't trust that my input matters."
- "I've been burned before."
- "This isn't a space where I feel safe being myself."

In multicultural environments, especially where power imbalances or past discrimination exist, this silence can become institutionalized.
But if you respond to silence not with impatience, but with curiosity—then you become the kind of leader people start opening up to.

**Empathy + Timing = Strategic Listening**

Empathy without timing is noise. Timing without empathy is manipulation.

But when you *listen with intention, speak with awareness,* and *create patterns where feedback becomes culture,* you unlock the deepest level of leadership: **influence without force.**

You won't need to push people. They'll walk with you.

You won't need to extract information. It'll come freely.

You won't need to constantly check in. Trust will become the medium you work in.

**In Practice: A Listening Ritual to Steal**

Want a practical habit to build this muscle?

Try the "Three-Minute Rule" once a week in your team meetings:

1. **Pick a topic**: What's one thing we're avoiding, one thing we're unsure of, or one thing that isn't working?
2. **Set a timer for 3 minutes.**
3. **Let anyone speak freely without interruption.** No rebuttals. No corrections. Just listening.
4. **Rotate the speaker. Repeat weekly.**

You'll be amazed how fast truth—and trust—start flowing.

Leading With Liberty: How to Lead in a Multicultural World

**Case Study: Bill Gates and the Precision of Listening at Scale**
**Background**

36

## Case Study: Bill Gates and the Precision of Listening at Scale

### Background

In the early 1980s, Microsoft was no longer just a scrappy startup. It was growing into a dominant force in the emerging personal computing revolution. But as the company scaled, so did the complexity—of decisions, of teams, and of communication.

And in the middle of this whirlwind was Bill Gates: a visionary known for his intellect, intensity, and—perhaps less famously—his calculated quiet.

While Gates is remembered for his bold strategies, what actually fueled Microsoft's momentum was his ability to **listen with timing, empathy, and precision.**

### Step 1: Listening as a Strategic Tool

From the outside, Gates often appeared curt or hyper-rational. But internally, he was known for something else entirely: **hearing what others missed.** His team recalls how he would sit silently in meetings, jotting notes, then ask one pointed question that shifted the entire direction of a product.

He didn't speak to dominate. He listened to detect leverage.

"If you can't summarize someone's idea better than they can," Gates once told a product manager,
"you haven't really understood it."

This wasn't just intellectual discipline. It was empathy in action: the kind that turns an engineer's buried insight into a billion-dollar innovation.

### Step 2: The Feedback Flywheel

Gates institutionalized strategic listening across Microsoft, especially with product users. He would read direct customer letters—sometimes hundreds per week—and flag them for his executive team. Not because it made for good PR, but because he knew **truth travels fastest from the frustrated.**

He once insisted the Excel team rewrite an entire interface after reviewing a handful of letters from power users. The team protested—"It's just a few complaints." Gates replied:
"If they took the time to write, there are a hundred more who didn't."
This became a foundational principle:
**Silence is data. Frustration is signal. Listening is strategy.**

### Step 3: The Think Week as Listening Ritual

Perhaps Gates' most famous leadership innovation was the *Think Week*: seven uninterrupted days alone in a cabin, reading hundreds of whitepapers, emails, and memos submitted by Microsoft employees from every level of the company.

This wasn't a retreat—it was a ritual of humility.
It told employees: **Your voice matters, even if I don't know your name.**

Ideas like Internet Explorer and .NET were born from these

sessions—not top-down strategy, but bottom-up curiosity. Gates didn't just listen. He **created time to listen.** He made it structural.

## Step 4: Empathy + Timing = Influence

Gates wasn't warm in the traditional sense. But his empathy came through in timing. He knew *when* to speak, and *when not to*:

- When a young engineer hesitated to challenge a flawed plan, Gates paused the meeting and asked them directly for input—turning that moment into a career-defining pivot.

- When teams hit internal conflict, he didn't play referee. He asked the deeper question: *What problem are we trying to solve, and what are we afraid to say?*

In this, Gates embodied the *Lead With Liberty* approach:
He didn't lead by volume or charisma. He led by **creating psychological airspace**—especially for dissent.

"My job isn't to be right," Gates once told his COO.
"It's to make sure we're not wrong for too long."

## Results: Listening as Leverage

By the time Gates stepped down as CEO:

- Microsoft had become the most influential tech company in the world.

- It had outmanoeuvred larger players by acting faster—not because it moved recklessly, but because it **listened earlier.**

- Employees described a culture where the smartest idea won—not the loudest voice.

## Why This Case Study Matters for Strategic Listening in Multicultural Teams

Gates proved that:

- You don't need to be touchy-feely to lead with empathy.

- You don't need to agree with everyone to hear them deeply.

- You don't need to shout to be heard—*you need to listen strategically.*

In multicultural teams, where assumptions abound and norms clash, Gates' model shines:

- **Decode silence.**

- **Spot tension before it sparks.**

- **Make space for voices that don't self-promote.**

- **Turn listening from courtesy into capability.**

Because in the end, liberty-driven leadership isn't just about protecting space—it's about **amplifying voice.**

### Apply the Gates Model: The "Think Hour"

Don't have a week? Start with an hour.
Each month, block 60 minutes to read anonymous team feedback,

customer reviews, and staff proposals—alone, undistracted.

End it by sending one message:

- "Here's what I heard."
- "Here's what I'll act on."
- "Here's who I'll follow up with."

**That's how strategic listening becomes cultural gravity.** And that's how you lead—on time, with empathy, and in liberty.

Here are five key lessons and principles from the chapter on Strategic Listening and the Bill Gates case study:

- **Listening Is a Strategic Skill, Not a Soft One**
  It's how leaders detect buried insights, unlock trust, and prevent conflicts—especially across cultural boundaries.

- **Silence Is Data—Decode It with Empathy**
  What's not said often matters more than what is; strategic leaders stay curious about quiet rooms and unspoken tensions.

- **Create Rituals That Make Listening Structural**
  From one-on-ones to anonymous feedback loops to "Think Hours," build habits that normalize speaking up and being heard.

- **Name the Elephant Before It Tramples the Room**
  Be the first to voice unspoken issues—not to control the narrative, but to create psychological safety for honest dialogue.

- **Empathy + Timing = Leadership Without Force**
  You don't need to dominate the room to influence it—you need to know when to ask, pause, or invite the right voice at the right moment.

42

# 5 SHARED NARRATIVES — COMMUNICATING CORE VALUES

In leadership, what you say *matters*—but *how* you say it often matters more.

You might have a vision worth following, a strategy that's sound, and a mission that serves liberty itself—but if your people don't *feel* it, don't *get* it, or can't *connect* with it, none of it will land.

That's where shared narratives come in. At their heart, shared narratives are *not* about slogans or brand statements. They are about translating values into the emotional languages of your people. And if you're leading a multicultural team—this is where the real work (and the real magic) happens.

**Communicate the Vision with Shared Values**

First, your vision must be anchored in values. Real ones. Not buzzwords.

- "We believe in ownership" beats "We want synergy."
- "We serve people who've been ignored by institutions" beats "We are customer-centric."
- "We want our users to feel dignity, not dependency" beats "We build efficient solutions."

Then, you weave those values into every communication—from weekly standups to major presentations to hiring interviews. You make it a drumbeat.

But don't stop there.

**When They Don't Get It, Go Where *They* Are**

Sometimes, even when you think you've nailed it—someone just doesn't get it.

Maybe it's a cultural gap. Maybe it's personality. Maybe it's just the way their brain is wired. This is your cue to *listen first*, not double down.

Here's the key principle: **When someone doesn't understand your values, don't just explain harder. Translate better.**

To do that, first understand *where they're coming from*. People carry with them worldviews shaped by:

- **Religion**
- **Philosophy**
- **Sports**
- **Military service**
- **Art**
- **Family upbringing**
- **National history**

These aren't just side-notes. These are the *lenses* through which they interpret everything.

If someone speaks in religious metaphors, meet them there:

- "This project isn't just work—it's a stewardship of trust."
- "We're building something that serves not just profit, but purpose."

If someone speaks in sports metaphors:

- "We've got the ball. We need to protect it until we score."
- "This is a team sport—no heroes, just assists."

If someone speaks in military terms:

- "We need discipline in execution, and clarity in command."
- "Every team member needs to know the mission objective."

This is not manipulation. It's *respectful translation*.

You're showing that you're not just listening to what they say—but how they say it. And when you do this well, something powerful happens:

**They start mirroring you back.**

Because when communication feels like a two-way bridge—not a broadcast tower—people begin to open up. They get honest. They drop the corporate mask and speak from experience. And that's when the real conversations—and real decisions—start happening.

**Why This Matters in Higher-Level Meetings**

This principle is not just for one-on-one conversations. It is *especially* useful in high-stakes meetings, boardrooms, strategic planning sessions—anywhere trust needs to scale fast.

Because in those rooms, people don't always say what they think. They posture. They play Défense. They code their language.

But if you speak *to their code*—you disarm the room.

- When a board member is concerned about risk but couches it in data, respond with evidence.
- When a stakeholder speaks in moral terms, meet them with values.
- When a partner speaks in metaphors of movement, change, or vision, reflect back in kind.

This shows respect. It shows understanding. And more than anything—it *builds influence without pressure*.

**From Metaphor to Meaningful Dialogue**

Once people feel heard in their native metaphor, they start getting *real*. They speak their truth—not the sanitized version. And when that happens, your job as a leader becomes easier and deeper:

- Problems surface *before* they explode.
- Ideas flourish *without* needing permission.
- Conflicts become *constructive*, not political.

People stop trying to "win" conversations, and start trying to solve the same problems—together.

**How to Practice This**

Here's a framework you can use:

1.  **Listen for Patterns**
    Over the next few meetings, start paying attention to the types of language people use.
    - Do they talk about "balance," "flow," "energy"? → Emotional language
    - "Structure," "metrics," "roadmaps"? → Systems thinking
    - "Calling," "service," "sacrifice"? → Moral or spiritual language
    - "Plays," "moves," "wins"? → Competitive or tactical language
2.  **Name and Reflect**
    Once you detect their communication mode, reflect back in that same mode. Even just one sentence can shift the dynamic.
3.  **Anchor in Shared Values**
    Whatever metaphor you use, always bring it back to the values that define your mission. That's the compass.
4.  **Invite Their Story**
    Ask them to tell a story about when they saw those values *in action*. Stories carry more weight than strategies.

**Final Word: Speak Human**

In a multicultural world, the challenge is not to erase difference, but to navigate it with skill and sincerity.

Shared narratives are not about reducing everything to lowest-common-denominator language. They're about building a high-trust, high-clarity, high-liberty space where people *want* to understand each other.

And that starts with you.

So next time you talk to your team, don't just ask: "Did they hear me?"

Ask: **"Did I speak in a way they feel?"**

Because once your values become *their* values—once your metaphors become *shared metaphors*—you're not just leading.

You're resonating.

46

**Case Study: Thomas Jefferson — Crafting a Universal Language of Liberty**

48

## Case Study: Thomas Jefferson — Crafting a Universal Language of Liberty

### Context

In 1776, the American colonies were fragmented—different economies, religions, cultures, and interests. The challenge wasn't just military or diplomatic—it was **narrative**. Jefferson had to write something that would unite farmers in Virginia, merchants in Boston, Quakers in Pennsylvania, and radicals in New York.

He didn't start with logistics. He started with **values**.

## Step 1: Anchor the Vision in Shared Values

Jefferson's draft of the Declaration didn't begin with grievances. It began with **a narrative anyone could feel**:

"We hold these truths to be self-evident, that all men are created equal…"

That wasn't just legal language. It was *moral clarity*.

He appealed not to British law or colonial tradition—but to **natural rights**, something bigger than governments and kings.

In doing so, Jefferson turned the idea of independence into a **moral mission**, not just a political rebellion.

## Step 2: Translate Across Worldviews

Jefferson knew he wasn't just writing for philosophers. He was writing for:

- **Christian congregations** who saw liberty as divine stewardship.
- **Enlightenment thinkers** who believed in reason and natural rights.
- **Everyday colonists** who just wanted fair treatment.

So, he borrowed language from **multiple traditions**:

- From **scripture**: "endowed by their Creator" → resonated with religious citizens.
- From **philosophy**: "life, liberty, and the pursuit of happiness" → inspired Enlightenment minds.
- From **human emotion**: words like "sufferance," "tyranny," and "usurpations" → created moral urgency.

He didn't just write *for* people—he wrote *as* if he *was* one of them, speaking in the metaphors and values they lived by.

## Step 3: Create a Repeating Drumbeat

Jefferson used **rhythmic structure** to make the values stick. The entire middle section of the Declaration follows a cadence:

"He has refused…"
"He has forbidden…"
"He has obstructed…"
"He has dissolved…"

This repetition-built momentum. It wasn't just rhetoric—it was *ritual*.

People could *feel* the injustice mounting. The values weren't abstract—they were visceral.

## Step 4: From Metaphor to Mobilization

By the end of the document, Jefferson moves from poetic values to **a clear, actionable conclusion**:

"…we mutually pledge to each other our Lives, our Fortunes and our sacred Honor."

That line hit like a drumbeat of solidarity.

It's the climax of shared narrative: not "I believe this," but **"We are in this together."**

### Why It Works for Multicultural Leadership

Even centuries later, Jefferson's declaration has been:

- Quoted by **civil rights leaders** (MLK's "I have a dream" speech explicitly references it).
- Used by **international freedom movements** as a template.
- Embraced by **citizens across political, racial, and philosophical lines**.

It's not because Jefferson solved every problem. It's because he created a **values-based story** so strong that people could **reinterpret it** and **expand it** over time.

### Leadership Lesson

Jefferson didn't demand alignment.

He **invited belonging**—through shared values, translated language, and timeless narrative.

And in doing so, he gave leaders throughout history a playbook on how to communicate liberty in ways people can not only understand—but **feel in their bones**.

Here are five key lessons and principles from the "Empowerment Through Value Creation" chapter and the Thomas Jefferson case study:

- **Value Creation Begins with Clarity, Not Commands**
  People align and contribute when they understand the real-world problem in human, relatable terms—not abstract goals.

- **Shared Values Bridge Cultural Differences**
  In multicultural teams, clearly communicated values create unity across backgrounds, beliefs, and worldviews.

- **Empowerment Is Built Through Systems, Not Slogans**
  Progress happens when people have clear goals, meaningful metrics, and feel their work genuinely impacts the mission.

- **Incentives Must Reflect Purpose, Not Just Pay**
  Align rewards—whether financial or symbolic—with outcomes that matter, to keep motivation high across sectors.

- **Narrative Is a Leadership Tool**
  Like Jefferson, great leaders use language, rhythm, and emotional clarity to turn individual effort into shared movement.

# 6 RADICAL TRANSPARENCY — BUILDING TRUST ACROSS DIVIDES

In a world that's fractured by misinformation, filtered narratives, and bureaucratic euphemisms, there's one thing that pierces through the fog like a beam of sunlight:

**Radical Transparency.**

This doesn't mean oversharing. It doesn't mean brutal honesty with no tact. It means leading from a place where **truth becomes the default**, not a privilege. Where **reality is a shared starting point**, not a disputed battlefield.

If you want trust to cross cultures, continents, and communication styles, radical transparency is not optional—it's *foundational*.

**Why Transparency Matters More in Multicultural Teams**

In multicultural settings, trust doesn't come pre-installed. You're dealing with people who may have:

- Lived through corrupt institutions.
- Worked in organizations where information was weaponized.
- Been marginalized and never told the full story.
- Been punished for asking questions.

So if your leadership feels vague, selective, or filtered—**they will fill in the gaps with fear.**

The antidote? **Be the most transparent person in the room.** Let that be your competitive advantage.

Transparency creates safety. Safety creates dialogue. Dialogue creates shared problem-solving. That's liberty in action.

**Face the Problem Head-On**

Radical transparency starts with one fundamental rule:

**Name the problem before it names you.**

Too many teams operate under a haze of unspoken issues:

- "We're not hitting targets"—but no one knows why.
- "People are leaving"—but exit interviews are buried.
- "Customer trust is down"—but the feedback loop is broken.

If your goal is to lead in liberty, you must cultivate a culture where **facing reality is not feared—it's expected**.

Instead of saying:

"We're exploring areas for optimization,"

Say: "We're behind on delivery and need to realign expectations. Here's the data."

Instead of saying:

"We're undergoing strategic restructuring,"

Say: "We've made mistakes in team structure that hurt morale. Here's how we're fixing it."

The truth is rarely what breaks a team. **What breaks a team is when the leader pretends everything's fine.**

**Set the Expectation: Truth Over Comfort**

Let your team know early and often: *we don't do false comfort here.*

That doesn't mean you're callous. It means you respect them enough to give them the truth—because only with the full picture can people make informed, liberated choices.

People don't just work for money. They work for **meaning**. And meaning requires **clarity**.

If you sugarcoat, you're robbing your team of the chance to truly *own* the mission. But if you're honest, even about the hard things, you unlock one of the most powerful tools in leadership: **collective courage.**

**Operationalize Transparency**

Radical transparency can't be a buzzword. It must be built into the operations of your team. Here's how:

1.  **Weekly "What's Not Working" Review**

    A no-blame, no-punishment space where the team openly shares what's broken—technically, culturally, or strategically. No finger-pointing, just Candor.

2.  **Transparent Dashboards**

    Share metrics—good and bad—with everyone. Revenue, user growth, attrition, feedback scores. Let people see the real scoreboard.

3.  **Post-Mortems Without Politics**

    When a project fails or underperforms, analyse it *together*. Invite people from every layer of the organization. Not to assign blame—but to learn faster.

4.  **Truth Walls**

    Have a shared space (digital or physical) where anyone can anonymously post uncomfortable truths or critical feedback. Review and respond publicly.

5.  **Real Talk at All-Hands**

    Your company-wide meetings should include a segment where leadership says:

    - "Here's where we're winning."
    - "Here's where we're failing."
    - "Here's what's next."

    Every time.

**Culture of Truth = Culture of Trust**

When you make transparency the norm:

- People stop hoarding information.
- Feedback becomes normalized.
- Silos collapse.
- Teams move faster because no one's walking on eggshells.

- You attract and retain people who value autonomy, responsibility, and courage—the heart of liberty.

Transparency doesn't just make communication easier. It makes your mission more *believable*.

**When Transparency Gets Tough**

There will be moments when the truth hurts:

- A major client walks away.
- The budget won't stretch far enough.
- A beloved leader behaves poorly.
- A bold experiment fails publicly.

In those moments, the temptation is to soften, to spin, to delay. But this is when you double down.

Your team is watching. If you're honest in the fire, they'll trust you in the rebuild.

Say:

- "This is a hit. We didn't expect it. But we'll own it, and here's how we move forward."
- "There was a breach of values. It hurts, but we must stand by what we say we believe."
- "This idea failed. Not because we're dumb—but because we're bold. That's the cost of real innovation."

Radical transparency is not about being right all the time. It's about being *real* all the time.

**Final Word: Liberty Begins With Truth**

In a multicultural world, where assumptions can lead to breakdowns, where silence can be interpreted as secrecy, and where trust is earned slowly but lost instantly—radical transparency is the great equalizer.

It says:

- "We're not perfect, but we're honest."
- "We don't have all the answers, but we won't hide the questions."
- "We're in this together, and we'll face the truth together."

That's what liberty-based leadership looks like.

**Radical transparency is not a tactic. It's a trust-building revolution.**

So step into the light—your team will follow.

56

### Case Study: Nelson Mandela — Telling the Truth That Could Heal a Nation

### Case Study: Nelson Mandela — Telling the Truth That Could Heal a Nation

When Nelson Mandela became President of South Africa in 1994, he inherited a country deeply fractured by apartheid—a regime built on secrecy, censorship, and institutionalized mistrust. Different groups had vastly different experiences, histories, and fears. If ever there was a test case for radical transparency—it was this.

Mandela knew that political power wasn't enough. What South Africa needed was **emotional legitimacy**, and that could only come through truth.

### Step 1: Naming the Pain Publicly

Mandela didn't try to paper over the past. He didn't call it "unrest" or "a complicated history." He **named apartheid for what it was**—a system of oppression and racial domination.

Instead of hiding behind diplomatic language, he opened his presidency with a message that honoured suffering, acknowledged wrongdoing, and set the tone for **truth as a foundation of unity**.

"Our nation has been robbed of its birthright, and today we claim it back—not with vengeance, but with honesty."

This public stance wasn't politically safe—but it was **morally necessary**.

### Step 2: Institutionalizing Transparency — The Truth and Reconciliation Commission

Mandela helped create one of the most groundbreaking models of radical transparency in modern leadership:

**The Truth and Reconciliation Commission (TRC)**.

Instead of secret trials or show trials, the TRC:

- Invited **perpetrators to tell the full truth**—in public, with full detail.

- Allowed **victims to share their stories**—in their own voices, often for the first time.

- Offered **amnesty not for silence, but for full disclosure**.

This was not comfortable. It was often heartbreaking. But it was revolutionary. It created a **shared reality** from previously siloed truths.

Mandela's message was clear:

"If we are to build a future together, we must face our past—together."

### Step 3: Leading by Example—Even When It Hurt

When Mandela faced criticism from allies—especially for reconciling with white South Africans, including former prison guards and apartheid officials—he didn't hide behind political spin. He told the truth:

"If I do not forgive, I will still be in prison."

He was transparent about the **emotional cost** of forgiveness, not just the political benefits. That honesty gave his leadership more depth and humanity. It wasn't just strategy—it was sincerity.

## Step 4: Truth as a Unifier in a Multicultural Nation

Mandela's South Africa was multilingual, multiracial, and filled with **deep mutual suspicion**. Radical transparency helped collapse those walls.

By refusing to sanitize the truth or weaponize it, Mandela turned **truth-telling into trust-building**:

- Truth gave victims dignity.
- Truth gave perpetrators a path to redemption.
- Truth gave the nation a way forward—not by forgetting, but by **facing together**.

## Leadership Lesson

Mandela showed that radical transparency isn't weakness.
It's what allows fractured people to become a **cohesive team**—not through forced unity, but through **shared honesty**.

## Why It Works for Liberty-Based Leadership

Mandela's model proves that liberty is not just about removing oppression—it's about **building systems of trust**.
And trust can only be built on truth.

He understood what many leaders miss:

- **Transparency creates dignity.**
- **Dignity creates dialogue.**
- **Dialogue creates a new culture.**

That's how you lead across divides.

Here are five key lessons and principles from **"Radical Transparency — Building Trust Across Divides"** and the **Nelson Mandela case study**:

- **Transparency Builds Trust, Especially Across Cultures**
  In diverse teams where past experiences may breed mistrust, consistent honesty creates psychological safety and shared understanding.

- **Name the Hard Truths Early and Clearly**
  Leaders must confront uncomfortable realities directly—because silence or spin breeds confusion, fear, and disconnection.

- **Operationalize Truth into Everyday Systems**
  Create structured, repeatable ways to surface, share, and act on truth—like dashboards, no-blame reviews, and open feedback channels.

- **Model Vulnerability as Strength**
  Like Mandela, great leaders show honesty not only when it's strategic—but when it's hard, personal, and real. That's how you build emotional legitimacy.

- **Truth-Telling Unifies, Even When It's Painful**
  Transparency transforms fractured communities into shared problem-solvers—by giving voice to all sides and inviting reconciliation over repression.

# 7 PROBLEM-FOCUSED CONFLICT RESOLUTION & ACCOUNTABILITY

**Conflict Is Inevitable—Blame Is Optional**
In any team, partnership, or organization, conflict is not a sign of failure. It's a sign that human beings are working together with diverse priorities, incentives, and perceptions. The danger lies not in conflict itself, but in how it's handled. Most failures stem not from the problem, but from personalizing it—assigning blame rather than responsibility.

**People Aren't Problems—Problems Are Problems**
When tension arises, the lazy route is to label someone:

- "They're not committed."
- "He's difficult."
- "She's just not a team player."

This mindset makes resolution nearly impossible. Why? Because **you can't hold someone accountable for being "difficult"**—that's a personality judgment, not a measurable behaviour. Instead, a principled approach demands that we isolate **the issue**, not the individual.

---

**The 3-Part Framework: Shift to Solutions**
1. **Define the Problem Objectively**
   - Wrong: "Jake keeps messing up the schedule."
   - Right: "The project schedule has slipped by three days due to late task submissions."
2. **Clarify Impact, Not Emotion**
   - Wrong: "It's frustrating when you don't follow up."
   - Right: "When follow-up is missed, it delays decisions by 48 hours, affecting delivery."
3. **Assign Clear Responsibility (Not Blame)**
   Ask:
   - Who owns the outcome?
   - Who supports that outcome?
   - What does success look like?

---

**Accountability Is About Agreements, Not Accusations**
Accountability is not about punishment. It's about **clarity**.
Here's a simple **Accountability Map** that defines roles:

| Role | Responsibility |
| --- | --- |
| **Owner** | Ultimate accountability for the task's success |
| **Contributors** | Provide input, resources, or approvals |

| Role | Responsibility |
| --- | --- |
| **Informed Parties** | Need updates but are not directly involved |

By assigning ownership clearly, ambiguity disappears. If everyone owns something, no one owns it. If roles are unclear, you don't get performance—you get polite chaos.

### A Real-World Example: From Blame to Clarity

Let's say your team failed to deliver a client report on time. Here's how the conversation usually goes:

**Blame-based:**

"Sarah didn't send her numbers again. This always happens."

Versus:

**Problem-focused:**

"The report was delayed because Q2 figures were submitted two days late. To avoid this next time, we'll assign the deadline to Sarah with a one-day buffer. Mark will send her a reminder 48 hours in advance."

Now you've:

- Isolated the issue
- Assigned responsibility
- Introduced a feedback loop

No one was attacked—but everyone was accountable.

### Principled Conflict Resolution

When conflict does emerge, use these ground rules:

1. **Focus on the facts.** What *specifically* happened or didn't happen?
2. **Name the gap.** What was the expectation, and what was the reality?
3. **Stay curious.** Ask: *What made sense to them at the time?*
4. **Collaborate forward.** Instead of rehashing mistakes, align on future-proof solutions.

This doesn't mean tolerating incompetence. It means **solving the root cause**, not just the symptom—or worse, the personality.

### The Liberty Ethos: Own Your Role, Respect Others'

A liberty-minded organization depends on voluntary association, mutual respect, and earned trust. That only works if each individual knows:

- What they own
- Where they support others
- How to speak truth without making enemies

Because in a free system, **clarity beats control**—and solving problems beats fixing people.

**Summary Takeaway:**
In conflict, forget who caused it. Focus on what caused it. Then make sure every person knows their role in fixing it.

65

**Case Study: Jefferson, Madison, and the Creation of the Supreme Court as the Highest Order**

67

**Case Study: Jefferson, Madison, and the Creation of the Supreme Court as the Highest Order**

**Background**

In the early years of the American republic, the question of how to handle conflict within the new government was a central challenge. The system of governance outlined by the Constitution was intended to balance power, prevent tyranny, and foster cooperation among states and individuals. However, there were disagreements among the framers regarding the roles and authority of the various branches of government.

Thomas Jefferson and James Madison, two of the most influential figures in shaping the United States, had differing views on the scope and power of the federal government, especially in terms of judicial authority. Their philosophical differences came to a head in the formation of the Supreme Court and its role in resolving conflicts and maintaining accountability.

**The Problem**

After the ratification of the U.S. Constitution, one of the most significant issues was how the new government would manage disputes among states, the federal government, and citizens. The framers had established the federal judiciary to provide a system of checks and balances, but the exact authority of this judiciary, especially the Supreme Court, remained unclear. Jefferson, with his vision of a limited federal government, was concerned that a strong judicial branch could usurp state power and infringe on the liberties of the people. Madison, while sharing Jefferson's belief in limiting federal authority, saw the judiciary as an essential counterbalance to the potential overreach of the legislative and executive branches. This philosophical tension would play out over the creation of the Supreme Court and its evolving role in conflict resolution.

**Defining the Problem Objectively**

The key issue was how to structure a judiciary that could adjudicate disputes effectively while respecting the principles of limited government. The creation of the Supreme Court as the highest order in the judicial system was a solution to prevent conflicts from escalating into constitutional crises, yet there was a clear concern about ensuring the Court did not gain too much power.

**Wrong Approach:** "Madison and Jefferson can't agree on how much power the Supreme Court should have."

**Right Approach:** "The debate centers on whether the judiciary should have the authority to overrule state laws or merely act as an impartial arbiter in disputes between state and federal powers."

**Clarifying Impact, Not Emotion**

As tensions between Jefferson and Madison grew, both men acknowledged the necessity of an independent judiciary. However, Jefferson's concern was that a judiciary unchecked by the states could lead to a consolidation of federal power, undermining the autonomy of state governments and the liberty of their citizens.

**Wrong Approach:** "Jefferson thinks the judiciary will become tyrannical."
**Right Approach:** "Jefferson is concerned that a powerful judiciary, particularly the Supreme Court, could interpret the Constitution in ways that extend federal authority at the expense of state sovereignty and individual liberties."

## Assigning Clear Responsibility

While Jefferson and Madison were aligned in their desire for a limited federal government, they had different ideas about how best to manage judicial conflicts. Madison, as a key proponent of the Constitution, recognized the importance of the Supreme Court in maintaining a system of checks and balances. Jefferson, on the other hand, feared the Court would be a tool for federal overreach.

**Who Owns the Outcome?** The ultimate responsibility for establishing the judicial branch and ensuring it functioned as intended lay with the legislative branch, particularly Congress, and the president, who had the power to nominate justices.

**Who Supports the Outcome?** Jefferson and Madison supported a judicial system that was fair, independent, and kept the federal government in check.

**What Does Success Look Like?** A successful outcome would be a judiciary that could resolve disputes impartially, upholding the Constitution without infringing on states' rights or personal liberties.

## Accountability Is About Agreements, Not Accusations

In the debate over the judiciary's role, both Jefferson and Madison realized that a system of accountability was necessary to prevent either branch of government from overstepping its bounds. The solution was not to destroy the idea of a powerful judiciary, but to ensure that the judiciary was accountable through checks and balances.

The Judiciary Act of 1789, which established the framework for the Supreme Court and the lower federal courts, was a critical step in formalizing this accountability. While Jefferson disagreed with some of the Act's provisions, particularly the expansion of judicial authority, both he and Madison ultimately understood that the judiciary must have enough power to fulfill its constitutional role without becoming a tool of government tyranny.

## A Real-World Example: From Blame to Clarity

In 1803, the conflict over judicial power came to a head with the landmark case *Marbury v. Madison*. This case solidified the principle of judicial review, allowing the Supreme Court to declare laws unconstitutional. While Jefferson feared that this decision would give the judiciary unchecked power, Madison recognized the necessity of an independent judiciary to uphold the Constitution.

**Blame-based Approach:** "Jefferson blames the judiciary for undermining states' rights and personal liberties."

**Problem-focused Approach:** "The judiciary's role is to ensure that laws align with the Constitution. The issue lies not with the Court itself, but with the balance of power between branches of government."

In *Marbury v. Madison*, Chief Justice John Marshall established judicial review, reinforcing the role of the Supreme Court as the final arbiter of constitutional disputes. This ruling demonstrated that conflict in the government could be resolved through an institutional process that respected both the need for a strong federal government and the protection of state and individual rights.

## Principled Conflict Resolution

Jefferson and Madison's philosophical conflict was ultimately resolved through a principled approach to governance. They recognized that, while they had differing views on the scope of federal power, they both understood the necessity of a judiciary that could resolve disputes and hold the government accountable.

The resolution of this conflict laid the groundwork for the functioning of the Supreme Court as the highest order in the American legal system. The Court would not only resolve conflicts between the federal and state governments but also ensure that the government operated within the bounds of the Constitution.

## The Liberty Ethos: Own Your Role, Respect Others'

In a liberty-minded system, each branch of government must know its role and respect the roles of others. The judiciary, in its role as the final arbiter, must balance its duty to uphold the Constitution with a respect for the powers and rights of the other branches. In a free society, clarity beats control, and solving systemic problems beats fixing individuals.

## Summary Takeaway:

The conflict between Jefferson and Madison over the creation of the Supreme Court and its role in resolving conflicts was not about personal animosities but about philosophical differences regarding the proper balance of power. Through principled conflict resolution, they ensured that the judiciary would function as an impartial arbiter, maintaining accountability without infringing on the liberties of the people or the authority of the states.

Here are five core lessons from **"Problem-Focused Conflict Resolution & Accountability"** and the **Jefferson–Madison case study** that distill the essence of liberty-aligned leadership:

- **Separate People from Problems**
  Labelling someone as "difficult" blocks resolution. Focus on behaviours and outcomes—not personalities—to create space for accountability without shame.

- **Accountability = Clarity, Not Control**
  Clearly define roles: who owns the outcome, who supports, and who needs to be informed. Without this, you get polite chaos, not progress.

- **Fix Systems, Not Scapegoats**
  Shift from blame to root-cause thinking. Ask: *What caused this?* not *Who messed up?* Resolution comes from process improvement, not personal judgment.

- **Use Conflict to Clarify Philosophy**
  Like Jefferson and Madison, don't avoid tension—use it to sharpen principles. Disagreements, when framed well, strengthen the system rather than fracture it.

- **Principled Conflict Builds Liberty**
  True liberty requires systems where disagreements are resolved through transparent, fair mechanisms—where truth guides

73

74

# 8 DEFENDING OPENNESS: COUNTERING INTOLERANCE

"Unlimited tolerance must lead to the disappearance of tolerance. If we extend unlimited tolerance even to those who are intolerant… then the tolerant will be destroyed, and tolerance with them."
— *Karl Popper, The Open Society and Its Enemies (1945)*

### Freedom Is Not Fragile—But It Does Require Defence

Openness is the backbone of any thriving institution—whether a company, a think tank, or a constitutional republic. But openness is not naivety. **An open society is not a society without boundaries—it's one with principled ones.** We welcome disagreement, diverse opinions, and even uncomfortable truths. But we **draw the line** at behaviours and ideologies that threaten the very ground rules of the open exchange: mutual respect, voluntary cooperation, and individual dignity.

### The Threat: Intolerance in the Guise of Principle

In modern organizations and public institutions, intolerance rarely marches in wearing jackboots. It often comes dressed as righteousness:

- "This viewpoint is dangerous, so we must silence it."
- "Their idea doesn't belong because they don't have the right background."
- "You must believe this—or you're against us."

These are not debates. These are power grabs masquerading as morality.

**This is how idea meritocracy gets hijacked.**

### What Is Idea Meritocracy?

Idea meritocracy means the **best idea wins**—not the loudest, the most senior, or the most popular. Ideas are weighed on evidence, logic, and principle—not emotion or social clout. But when intolerance seeps in, this process becomes corrupted. People start **punishing dissent,** and instead of improving the system, they aim to control it.

**How to Defend Openness Without Becoming Oppressive**
Here's the principled playbook:

**1. Call Out the Value Breach, Not the Person**
Wrong:
"You're being intolerant and toxic."
Right:
"You're pushing to silence a view rather than challenge it with reason. That violates our core value of open dialogue."

This avoids moralizing and sticks to the **shared standard** everyone agreed to upon entering the organization. It reframes the moment as a **breach of process**, not a personal failure.

**2. Show the Impact—With Full Transparency**
Transparency isn't just for data; it's for behaviour. When intolerance attempts a takeover, **shine the lights**:

- Show how open dialogue has historically solved hard problems.
- Reveal the chilling effect suppressing ideas has had on others.
- Present feedback from teammates who feel stifled.

Most people don't want to be the villain. They may not even realize they've become one. **Transparency disarms the story they tell themselves** and gives them a chance to realign.

**3. Offer a Principled Exit**
If someone continues to push against the organization's commitment to openness—be it through censorship, ideological purity tests, or public shaming—then clarity is mercy:

"If you feel you can no longer support our value of open exchange, we respect that. You're free to seek an environment more aligned with your principles. But this is what we stand for."

You're not cancelling anyone. You're **offering the front door—** politely, clearly, and without drama.

**4. In Public Institutions: Consequences Must Be Formal**
In public office, where officials are **entrusted by the people**, intolerance must not just be discouraged—it must be formally addressed.

When an official undermines the core civic values of open debate, due process, and equal rights, they don't just endanger their own credibility—they endanger the institution.

In these cases:

- Make the behaviour public and factual.
- Show how it violates constitutional duties or public trust.
- Initiate formal procedures: **ethics hearings, censure, or impeachment**, if warranted.

Not to punish—but to **preserve the integrity of the system**.

---

### The Cost of Inaction

Tolerance of intolerance leads to cultural decay. People stop speaking up. Ideas get filtered before they're shared. Innovation dies. Civility dies. And eventually—freedom dies.

Popper was not warning us to become censors. He was warning us to become **guardians of the framework that makes freedom work**.

---

### Final Word: Openness with Teeth

Defending openness isn't soft. It's steel in principle, velvet in tone. It means:

- **Welcoming all ideas—until they demand we silence others.**
- **Giving people a way to course-correct—before removing them with clarity.**
- **Standing by values so openly that those who violate them self-select out.**

---

### Summary Takeaway:

Openness is not weakness. It's strength with a moral spine.
Intolerance doesn't just violate a rule—it poisons the well.
And if they won't stop poisoning it, show them the door before they burn the place down.

78

**Case Study: Winston Churchill's Leadership in Defending Openness During World War II**

Leading With Liberty: How to Lead in a Multicultural World

## Case Study: Winston Churchill's Leadership in Defending Openness During World War II

### Context: The Battle for Public Discourse and National Unity (1940s)

In the 1940s, as Nazi Germany under Adolf Hitler's regime posed a direct threat to the very existence of Britain, the world was witnessing a rise in the perils of ideological extremism. Yet, within Britain's own ranks, divisions emerged regarding the extent to which the government should respond to this global crisis. Winston Churchill, then the British Prime Minister, confronted internal and external intolerance with a commitment to defending openness, unity, and free dialogue—principles rooted in classical liberal thought.

Churchill had to navigate multiple tensions: disagreements within his own government, debates in the press, and the increasing influence of ideological movements that threatened the values of democracy, free speech, and open governance. Despite these internal challenges, Churchill defended the principles of open dialogue and national unity against forces of intolerance in a way that upheld the integrity of Britain's open society.

## Step 1: Call Out the Value Breach, Not the Person

As war loomed large, Churchill had to face voices within his own Cabinet and Parliament who favoured appeasement with Hitler, notably Neville Chamberlain and other appeasers who believed Britain could avoid war by conceding to Nazi demands. These individuals argued that the Nazi regime could be reasoned with, undermining the national Défense strategy.

Rather than personally attacking these appeasers, Churchill reframed the argument to focus on the **core value of national survival and the integrity of Britain's values**:

"We must never surrender to the intolerable force of tyranny. The price of appeasement is not just the security of our borders, but the very soul of our country."

Churchill's focus was not on vilifying his peers but on defending the fundamental right of the British people to determine their future without the shadow of dictatorship. His eloquent arguments, grounded in **reason**, highlighted the dangerous consequences of silencing open debate and capitulating to tyranny.

## Step 2: Show the Impact—With Full Transparency

Throughout the war, Churchill faced strong opposition, including the media, which became divided over the government's strategies. Some outlets and figures on the left and right of the political spectrum criticized his decision to declare war, leading to public fear, division, and misinformation.

Instead of retreating into secrecy or relying on censorship, Churchill made a clear point of showing **how openness and transparency in communication were vital to Britain's survival**. In his famous radio broadcasts, he regularly spoke directly to the British people:

"The battle of Britain is not just fought in the air—it is fought in the hearts and minds of every citizen. Every blow struck against tyranny is a blow for liberty. This is the price of freedom, and it cannot be achieved in silence."

By using transparency, Churchill not only inspired confidence but also highlighted how any form of intolerance—whether from Nazis or appeasers—threatened the survival of free speech and open discourse. He emphasized that the **cost of inaction** would be greater than the conflict itself.

## Step 3: Offer a Principled Exit

Churchill's political rivals, particularly those who still favoured appeasement, began to feel increasingly marginalized as his position grew stronger. Rather than resorting to punitive measures or political infighting, Churchill offered a **principled exit** to those who could not align with Britain's wartime values of resistance and freedom.

He famously invited any members of the government who disagreed with the direction of the war effort to leave, rather than forcing them into conformity. In one such instance, when Lord Halifax, a prominent advocate of negotiation with Hitler, considered stepping down, Churchill expressed:

"If you cannot support the war effort with all your heart, I will not ask you to remain in office. But you must respect our shared duty to the nation."

By doing so, Churchill allowed opponents to disengage on their own terms, preserving the integrity of the government and maintaining clarity in the mission to defeat Nazi Germany. He demonstrated that **defending openness does not require silencing dissent—it requires principled separation when core values are breached.**

## Step 4: In Public Institutions: Consequences Must Be Formal

Churchill did not hesitate to take formal action when necessary. This included publicly addressing acts of treason or ideological extremism. When individuals or groups within the British establishment openly undermined the war effort or sympathized with Nazi ideology, he ensured that consequences were formal and visible, including legal actions and public accountability.

This culminated in the **expulsion of fascist sympathizers** from public office and institutions, including prominent figures like Sir Oswald Mosley, the leader of the British Union of Fascists. While Churchill believed in free speech, he also recognized the necessity of protecting the institutions of liberty and open dialogue from those who would pervert them.

## Outcome: A United Nation Defending Freedom

Winston Churchill's leadership during this period is a case study in **defending openness while countering intolerance**. He rejected the idea of silencing opponents simply because they disagreed with him. Instead, he focused on defending the **framework of democratic principles and free discourse**, even in the face of those who sought to undermine or destroy it.

Under Churchill's leadership, Britain maintained its commitment to freedom of speech and open exchange, even as the nation faced the most intense external threats. His ability to **call out breaches of core values** with dignity, show the **impact of intolerance**, and provide a **principled exit** for those unwilling to defend these values allowed Britain to remain united.

---

### Leadership Lesson

Churchill's approach teaches that defending openness is not about passively tolerating any and all ideas, but about standing firm in defence of **liberty, respect, and reasoned discourse**. In the face of intolerance, it is critical to ensure that the framework of openness is protected—not just for the sake of tolerance but for the survival of the very system that allows freedom to flourish.

In a world where ideological purity tests and efforts to silence dissent are increasingly common, Churchill's ability to **defend openness without becoming oppressive** serves as a model of principled leadership.

Here are five key lessons and leadership principles from **"Defending Openness: Countering Intolerance"** and the **Winston Churchill case study**:

- **Openness Requires Boundaries to Survive**
  Tolerance doesn't mean accepting everything—it means protecting the conditions that allow open discourse, including mutual respect, voluntary cooperation, and individual dignity.

- **Challenge Intolerance by Reframing, Not Attacking**
  Focus on how actions breach shared values—not on demonizing individuals. This maintains clarity without escalating conflict.

- **Use Transparency to Reveal, Not Just Inform**
  Shine a light on how intolerance suppresses dialogue and innovation. Real transparency shows the *impact* of behaviour, not just the facts.

- **Offer Exit Paths for Ideological Misalignment**
  When individuals violate core values repeatedly, give them a clear, respectful choice: align with the mission—or step away. Openness does not mean endless tolerance for undermining it.

- **Protect Institutions Through Principled Action**
  In public or civic settings, formal consequences are necessary to preserve the integrity of open systems. Liberty must be defended not only in spirit—but in structure.

86

# 9 CONTINUOUS GROWTH: FEEDBACK LOOPS & LONG-TERM PROGRESS

**Growth Isn't a Destination. It's a Loop.**

Progress in any organization—be it a startup, a civic institution, or a philosophical movement—is not linear. It doesn't come from grand gestures or single wins. It comes from **continuous iteration**, **feedback**, and **course correction**. That's the loop.

But for that loop to work, everyone must agree—**consciously or not—to play the long game.**

### Enter Game Theory: Why Growth Is a Repeated Game

In game theory, a **Nash Equilibrium** is the point in a game where no player has anything to gain by changing their strategy, assuming others stick to theirs. Everyone has found a kind of stable "truce."

In a **one-time game**, short-term wins matter. But in a **repeated game**—which is what life, work, and community are—**long-term cooperation is the only winning strategy**.

This is how trust, innovation, and resilience are built. Everyone plays their part. Everyone assumes good faith. Everyone stays in the loop.

### What Happens When Someone Deviates?

Deviating from the equilibrium—by undermining trust, withholding feedback, gaming the system, or acting only for short-term personal gain—doesn't just hurt the immediate moment. It **breaks the loop**.

In repeated games, when one player breaks trust, the others retaliate or withdraw. This leads to a classic outcome:

**Mutually Assured Destruction.**

The game becomes toxic. People stop collaborating. Progress halts. And even the short-term "winner" loses long-term standing.

### The 3-Strikes Framework: Humane Accountability

We don't expect perfection—but we do expect **pattern recognition**.

So here's how principled organizations handle deviation in a **growth-first, human-first** way:

### 1st Deviation: Curiosity, Not Condemnation

"Hey, it looks like something in this process didn't align. Want to talk through what happened?"

This assumes **good intent** and invites honesty. No shame. Just a reset.

### 2nd Deviation: Clarify Consequences

"We're seeing the same issue crop up again. It's disrupting momentum and affecting others. Let's align on expectations moving forward."

Now we shift from observation to clear, collaborative standards. We document, we agree, and we re-enter the game.

### 3rd Deviation: Show the Breach of Equilibrium

At this point, the message is stronger—but still principled:

"You've now stepped outside the system we're all part of. This game only works if we all play by the same rules. If you keep breaking the loop, we all lose—including you."

Here, the **Nash Equilibrium is made explicit**. You're not punishing them—you're **offering clarity**. You're reminding them that deviation isn't about them versus the system—it's about **everyone's progress at stake**.

### The Long Game Requires Long Memory

Feedback loops are not surveillance. They're how we **learn, adjust, and grow**—together.

They say trust takes years to build and seconds to break. But in a culture of continuous feedback, we **build faster, break less, and bounce back better**. Feedback isn't friction—it's fuel.

### Rebuilding the Loop

If someone does breach the loop multiple times and chooses not to course-correct, that's a choice. And with every choice comes consequence.

But we still offer a principled path:

- **Exit with integrity** if values no longer align.
- **Redeem with commitment** if growth is truly desired.

No shaming. No blacklists. But no illusions either.

### Final Word: Progress Isn't Passive

Continuous growth isn't just something we experience—it's something we protect. The feedback loop isn't fragile. But it is sacred. And defending it means understanding the game we're playing:

If we all play the long game, everyone wins.

But if enough players defect, we all lose.

### Summary Takeaway:

Growth is a repeated game. Play it with transparency, feedback, and fairness.

Deviate once—we learn.

Deviate twice—we align.

Deviate thrice—you've chosen to step outside the loop.

89

Leading With Liberty: How to Lead in a Multicultural World

Leading With Liberty: How to Lead in a Multicultural World

**Case Study: Toyota's Continuous Improvement (Kaizen) and Long-Term Growth**

92

**Case Study: Toyota's Continuous Improvement (Kaizen) and Long-Term Growth**

**Context: The Foundation of Toyota's Growth Philosophy**

Toyota's rise to prominence in the automobile industry isn't the result of a few grand achievements or breakthroughs. Instead, it is the product of continuous, incremental improvement—a philosophy deeply embedded in its culture and business practices. This commitment to **continuous growth** and **feedback loops** has been the cornerstone of Toyota's success for decades. Known as **Kaizen**—the Japanese term for "continuous improvement"—Toyota's approach reflects the principles of long-term cooperation and iterative progress rather than short-term gains.

**Step 1: Feedback Loops as the Core of Continuous Improvement**

At the heart of Toyota's business is its **Toyota Production System (TPS)**, which is built on constant feedback loops between management, workers, and processes. TPS incorporates both **process improvement** and **employee involvement** at all levels. The system's success lies in its emphasis on small, ongoing improvements, often made by workers who are closest to the production processes.

**Key Example: The Role of Team Leaders and Employees**

In Toyota's assembly lines, team leaders are empowered to stop the production line when they notice a problem or inefficiency. The team is then expected to discuss the issue, identify the root cause, and implement a solution—often making small adjustments to the process. This feedback loop is not about finding blame but about **improving the system and preventing future errors**. It creates a culture where **everyone plays a role in the growth and success of the company**.

The feedback system allows Toyota to identify inefficiencies early, before they spiral into bigger problems, ensuring **long-term resilience** and the constant improvement of both products and processes. For example, in response to early issues with vehicle quality, Toyota implemented regular "kaizen events" where employees across different departments worked together to identify opportunities for improvement. These changes weren't drastic but cumulative, leading to the overall improvement of quality and production efficiency.

**Step 2: Game Theory and Long-Term Cooperation**

Toyota's approach mirrors the principles of **game theory**, where the company recognizes that sustainable growth isn't about **one-time victories** or isolated wins. Instead, it's about playing the **long game** of cooperation and improvement, where everyone in the organization understands their role and contributes to collective success.

The **Nash Equilibrium** in Toyota's case isn't about achieving a fixed solution—it's about maintaining the delicate balance of continuous feedback and iteration. If one part of the system deviates from this cycle, it can undermine the whole operation. When an employee or a department deviates from the cooperative approach, the company risks **mutually assured destruction**, leading to inefficiency, wasted resources, and frustration.

A prime example of this in Toyota's history was the company's response to early problems with the **TPS**—where managers had initially tried to force adherence to the production line rather than encouraging collaborative problem-solving. This resulted in bottlenecks, decreased morale, and suboptimal production outcomes. Toyota quickly recognized that **short-term efficiency goals** were less important than maintaining the long-term success of their **collaborative feedback loop**.

---

**Step 3: Humane Accountability in Continuous Growth**

Toyota's culture of feedback doesn't tolerate sustained deviations from the system. When issues arise, they don't simply punish employees or seek scapegoats. Instead, Toyota applies a **humane accountability model**, similar to the **3-Strikes Framework** for managing deviations:

1. **1st Deviation: Curiosity, Not Condemnation** When an employee or department strays from the process, management doesn't immediately react with punishment. Instead, they approach the issue with **curiosity** and an open mind. **"What happened here?"** is the first question, encouraging transparency and honesty.

Example: If a production line isn't meeting targets, managers work with workers to understand why. They ask about what challenges occurred, what worked, and what didn't. The goal isn't to place blame but to identify how to improve the system.

2. **2nd Deviation: Clarify Consequences** If the issue reoccurs, Toyota becomes more focused on **clarifying the consequences** of continued inefficiencies. At this stage, the company is still focused on **collaborative solutions**, but now there's a clear understanding that **not addressing the issue will lead to performance and productivity losses**.

Example: If an issue arises a second time, management holds a meeting with the team to **align on expectations** and introduce clearer guidelines or processes. This is when the "**standardization**" phase of the process comes into play—getting everyone on the same page.

3. **3rd Deviation: Show the Breach of Equilibrium** If an individual or group continually deviates from the process and refuses to cooperate, Toyota doesn't just ignore the breach. Instead, they **explicitly address the breach of the system**. This is not punitive, but it is clear.

Example: If a worker repeatedly bypasses standard procedures, a manager might say, "You're stepping outside the system we've all agreed to. If this continues, it will affect everyone's ability to meet their targets. It's in everyone's best interest to stick to the system, or we risk undermining the whole process."

---

**Step 4: Rebuilding the Loop**

When feedback loops are broken, Toyota doesn't treat the situation as a lost cause. Instead, they focus on **rebuilding the loop** through **redeeming**

**commitment** or allowing individuals to exit with integrity if the values no longer align. For example, when a senior manager fails to support the principles of TPS, Toyota encourages **recommitment to the process** or, if necessary, helps facilitate an **exit** in a dignified and constructive manner. This emphasis on **redeeming commitment** and **respecting integrity** shows that Toyota values **long-term growth** over short-term efficiency. The feedback process isn't about enforcing rigid rules but about **evolving together** toward shared goals.

## Final Word: Continuous Growth as a Strategic Advantage

Toyota's commitment to **continuous growth** isn't passive. It's an ongoing, iterative process driven by **feedback loops** that are actively protected and nurtured. By applying a **game-theory lens** to their operations, Toyota has ensured that long-term collaboration—rooted in mutual trust—is the only way to achieve **sustained progress**.

By integrating **humane accountability** and constantly adjusting the system, Toyota has built an environment where mistakes are **opportunities for growth**, not failures. This results in **feedback loops that accelerate progress**, ensuring that the company doesn't just stay competitive—it continually evolves to meet future challenges.

## Leadership Lesson

Toyota's approach teaches that **growth isn't a destination—it's a loop**. Sustainable success comes from an unwavering commitment to **continuous improvement**, where every member of the organization plays a role in the feedback process. The key to success is maintaining **cooperation and alignment** over the long term, ensuring that everyone stays committed to the shared values and goals that drive growth forward. By embracing **feedback as fuel**, rather than friction, Toyota has created an organization that can continually evolve, adapt, and thrive. **Continuous growth** is not just a strategic advantage—it's the path to long-term **resilience and success**.

Here are **five distilled leadership insights** from **"Continuous Growth: Feedback Loops & Long-Term Progress"** and the **Toyota case study**, built for clarity and real-world application:

- **Growth Is a Loop, Not a Leap**
  Sustainable progress comes from continuous feedback and iteration—not single breakthroughs. Every step forward is part of a repeated game that builds trust, not just results.

- **Trust Is the True Currency of Long-Term Play**
  When people deviate from shared norms, it doesn't just break a rule—it breaks the system. The feedback loop only works if everyone stays in the game with good faith.

- **Use Feedback as Fuel, Not Fire**
  Like Toyota's Kaizen, feedback should start with curiosity, escalate with clarity, and only shift to consequence when all else fails. No shame—just shared standards.

- **Apply the 3-Strikes Framework with Humanity**
  1st strike = Ask.
  2nd strike = Align.
  3rd strike = Address the system breach.
  Growth is for everyone, but accountability keeps the loop intact.

- **If the Loop Breaks, Rebuild—Or Release**
  When values no longer align, offer a dignified path out—or an invitation back in with real commitment. Feedback loops aren't prisons—they're partnerships.

# 10 OPEN-MIND INNOVATION: HARNESSING CULTURAL DIVERSITY

**Why Innovation Is Oxygen**

In any thriving organization—or nation—**innovation isn't a luxury; it's survival.**

It's how we solve new problems, grow beyond old paradigms, and stay a step ahead of stagnation.

That means **R&D (Research & Development)** isn't just a department. It's a mindset. A culture. A system.

And the fuel for that system? Not just money. Not just tech.

It's **people. Diverse people. Thinking freely, across boundaries.**

---

**The Power of Cultural & Cognitive Diversity**

When people from different backgrounds, mindsets, and disciplines collide—with openness and respect—ideas get sharper. Systems get better. Blind spots get exposed.

This is **idea meritocracy** on steroids.

But for that to work, there's a catch:

**People must be free to think differently—AND must be guided by shared constraints.**

Without freedom, you get conformity.

Without constraints, you get chaos.

But with both? You get breakthrough innovation.

---

**The Iron Triangle of Innovation: Pick Any Two**

Every innovation project—whether it's a new app, policy, or invention—lives inside the classic project triangle:

**Fast. Cheap. Good.**

Pick any two.

- Want it **fast and good**? It won't be cheap.
- Want it **cheap and fast**? It won't be good.
- Want it **good and cheap**? It'll take time.

Understanding this trade-off is key. It teaches innovators to **focus**, not flail.

And it pushes teams to **get creative under pressure**—which is where real magic happens.

---

**Divergent vs. Convergent Thinking: The Dynamic Duo**

Innovation requires **both rebels and refiners.** Here's how they differ:

| Divergent Thinkers | Convergent Thinkers |
| --- | --- |
| Generate wild ideas | Refine ideas into solutions |

| Divergent Thinkers | Convergent Thinkers |
| --- | --- |
| Break patterns | Find patterns |
| Thrive in ambiguity | Thrive in structure |
| Say: "Why not?" | Say: "What works?" |

A high-functioning culture doesn't choose one over the other. It **lets them collaborate—or even compete—within principled boundaries.** That's how you stay creative **and** constructive.

### Freedom Within a Framework

Open-minded innovation means:

- The **freedom to explore weird ideas**
- The **openness to hear unfamiliar perspectives**
- The **courage to be wrong without being punished**

...but also:

- **Time constraints** to push decisions
- **Budget caps** to spark creative resourcefulness
- **Quality standards** to protect users and reputation

"Give people a sandbox, not a cage."

Let them build. Let them play. Just let them know where the walls are.

### How to Foster a Culture of Open Innovation

1. **Celebrate useful failure.** Not every idea wins. But if we learned something fast? That's a victory.
2. **Reward curiosity, not just results.** Give credit to the question-askers, not just the closers.
3. **Mix minds across silos.** Put your engineers with your poets. Your analysts with your artists.
4. **Check your ego at the whiteboard.** If your idea loses in a fair debate, you still won—because the team got better.

### The Liberty Angle: Innovation Is Freedom in Motion

A society that fears failure cannot invent. A company that punishes nonconformity cannot adapt.

**Liberty is not just a value—it's a strategy.**

It lets people follow their hunches, test their intuitions, and **discover what works through action, not permission.**

But that liberty only thrives when people accept the **shared discipline** of constraints, deadlines, and quality.

### Final Word: Open-Mind, Clear Eyes, Limit-Driven Hands

Innovation doesn't happen by accident. It happens by giving people the right **to explore**—and the **responsibility to deliver.**

**Cultural diversity gives us the ideas.**
**Constraints give us the urgency.**
**Freedom gives us the courage.**
That's how innovation scales. That's how progress survives. And that's how liberty wins.

---

**Summary Takeaway:**
Innovation lives at the edge of liberty and limits.
Let people think differently—but anchor them with shared expectations.
That's not control. That's the contract of creation.

Leading With Liberty: How to Lead in a Multicultural World

Cultural diversity gives us the ideas.
Constraints give us the urgency.
Freedom gives us the courage.
That's how innovation scales. That's how progress survives. And that's how liberty wins.

Summary Takeaway:
Innovation lives at the edge of liberty and limits.
Let people think differently—but anchor them with shared expectations.
That's not control. That's the contract of creation.

**Case Study: Steve Jobs and the Power of Open-Mind Innovation**
**Context: Steve Jobs' Innovation Philosophy**

**Case Study: Steve Jobs and the Power of Open-Mind Innovation**
  **Context: Steve Jobs' Innovation Philosophy**
Steve Jobs, the co-founder of Apple Inc., revolutionized the technology industry through his ability to integrate **cultural diversity**, **open-minded innovation**, and **strategic constraints**. Jobs didn't just focus on developing new products; he fostered a culture of continuous growth, creativity, and perfectionism that transformed Apple from a garage startup into one of the most valuable and innovative companies in the world. His leadership embodies the principles of **open-minded innovation** and **cultural diversity**, proving that innovation thrives when ideas are both free and grounded in shared expectations.

**Step 1: Embracing Cultural and Cognitive Diversity**
Steve Jobs was known for surrounding himself with a team of individuals from various cultural and professional backgrounds. He understood that true innovation requires a **multidisciplinary approach**—a blend of diverse perspectives, experiences, and expertise. Jobs created a culture where **divergent thinking** (wild, unconventional ideas) and **convergent thinking** (refining those ideas into practical products) could thrive together.

**Key Example: The Development of the iPhone**
The creation of the **iPhone** serves as a prime example of how Jobs leveraged **cognitive diversity** within his teams. Engineers, designers, marketers, and even artists were brought together to create a device that combined technology, design, and usability in a way that had never been done before. Jobs encouraged his teams to **think differently**, bringing together **product designers** who understood user experience, **hardware engineers** who focused on device functionality, and **software engineers** who were able to develop an intuitive operating system.

The collaboration between individuals with diverse skill sets led to the creation of a product that was groundbreaking—not just for its technological innovation, but also for its **simplicity** and **design aesthetic**. Jobs famously integrated **beauty with functionality**, ensuring that both the external and internal components of the iPhone were crafted to work together in harmony.

**Step 2: The Balance of Freedom and Constraints**
One of Jobs' most famous beliefs was that innovation required a balance between **freedom to explore** and **constraints that guide focus**. He was known for creating an environment at Apple where teams had the freedom to innovate, but were also given clear boundaries within which to work.

**Key Example: The Development of the Macintosh**
The development of the **Macintosh** in the early 1980s was a prime

example of how Jobs used constraints to spark creativity. While Jobs allowed his team the freedom to experiment with innovative ideas, he set a clear goal: the **Macintosh** had to be **user-friendly, affordable**, and **compact**—all within a short timeframe and a limited budget. The pressure of these constraints forced the team to think creatively, leading to the design of one of the most iconic personal computers in history.

However, the most significant constraint was Jobs' unwavering focus on **simplicity**. He famously insisted that the Macintosh's interface should be so intuitive that anyone, regardless of technical knowledge, could use it. This constraint ultimately led to the development of the **graphical user interface (GUI)**, which was revolutionary at the time and became the standard for personal computers.

**Step 3: Divergent and Convergent Thinking in Action**

Jobs was known for encouraging both **divergent thinking** and **convergent thinking** in his teams. He believed that in order to create truly groundbreaking products, it was essential to **think outside the box**, while also refining and simplifying those ideas to make them feasible and user-friendly.

**Key Example: The iPod and the Music Industry**

When Apple set out to create the **iPod**, Jobs' team had to balance **divergent thinking**—coming up with new ways to disrupt the music industry—with **convergent thinking**—refining that concept into a practical, marketable device. Jobs famously combined **music, design, and technology** to create a product that was **easy to use** and **aesthetically pleasing**. But the iPod wasn't just a device; it was part of a larger vision that included the **iTunes Store**, which allowed users to purchase and download music legally and easily.

The iPod's success came not only from its technological innovation but from Jobs' ability to blend creative ideas (divergent thinking) with practical solutions (convergent thinking). He also made sure that every product detail, from the interface to the materials used, was **refined to perfection**.

**Step 4: Fostering a Culture of Open Innovation**

Steve Jobs created an environment at Apple where **failure was not feared** but embraced as part of the innovation process. He encouraged experimentation and risk-taking, knowing that **innovation involves trial and error**. However, he also established **clear standards** for success, ensuring that ideas weren't just pursued for the sake of novelty but had to meet Apple's high standards for design and usability.

**Key Example: The Apple "Think Different" Campaign**

One of Jobs' most famous mottos was **"Think Different"**, which encapsulated his philosophy on innovation. The **Think Different campaign** not only celebrated those who dared to be different (such as **Albert Einstein** and **Martin Luther King Jr.**) but also challenged the status quo, encouraging both Apple employees and consumers to embrace change and creativity.

Jobs believed that **celebrating failure** was key to innovation. If an idea didn't work, he saw it as an opportunity to learn and improve. The **failure of the Apple Newton**, an early attempt at a personal digital assistant (PDA), led to the development of the iPhone—a far more successful product that integrated the lessons learned from past failures.

### Step 5: The Liberty Angle—Innovation as Freedom in Motion

Jobs viewed innovation as **freedom in motion**—a process that thrived when individuals were given the **liberty** to explore new ideas without the constraints of traditional thinking. He believed that to truly innovate, you had to break free from conventional norms and think outside the box. However, that **freedom** was always balanced with a **commitment to excellence**, pushing his teams to constantly refine and improve.

#### Key Example: Apple's Product Ecosystem

Apple's ecosystem, where hardware, software, and services work seamlessly together, is a reflection of Jobs' belief that true innovation requires both **freedom to create** and **discipline to execute**. While Apple products like the **iPhone**, **iPad**, and **MacBook** are all distinct, they are also integrated into a larger system that offers a **consistent user experience**. This was only possible because Jobs understood the importance of working within a shared framework of **design, quality, and functionality**.

### Conclusion: Open-Mind, Clear Eyes, Limit-Driven Hands

Steve Jobs' approach to innovation shows that breakthrough success happens when **freedom and constraints** are balanced. He created an environment where employees had the freedom to **think differently** and pursue bold ideas, but also imposed **constraints**—in terms of design, quality, and time—that ensured these ideas were developed into **practical, world-changing products**.

Through his leadership, Apple consistently demonstrated that **innovation thrives at the edge of liberty and limits**—where diverse minds come together to solve problems and challenge the status quo, but are always grounded by clear expectations and shared goals.

### Leadership Lesson

Steve Jobs' leadership exemplifies how organizations can harness the power of **open-minded innovation** by embracing **cultural diversity**, giving teams the freedom to explore, while providing the structure needed to stay focused and deliver results. By combining **liberty with responsibility**, Jobs created a culture that allowed **Apple** to become a global leader in innovation.

**Summary Takeaway: Innovation thrives at the intersection of freedom and limits.** Allow your team the space to think differently, but anchor them with shared expectations and a commitment to excellence. This is the foundation of groundbreaking creativity and long-term success.

Here are **five key leadership insights** distilled from **"Open-Mind Innovation: Harnessing Cultural Diversity"** and the **Steve Jobs case study**, crafted for clarity, action, and inspiration:

- **Diversity Drives Breakthroughs**
  Innovation flourishes when different perspectives collide. Cultural and cognitive diversity aren't just virtues—they're engines of sharper thinking and smarter solutions.
- **Freedom Needs a Frame**
  Creativity without constraints is chaos. But limits without liberty are lifeless. Great leaders give their teams a sandbox— freedom to build, with boundaries that guide.
- **Balance Divergent + Convergent Thinking**
  The rebels dream. The refiners deliver. Both are essential. Don't just allow creative tension—engineer it into your culture.
- **Celebrate Curiosity, Learn from Failure**
  Innovation doesn't punish wrong turns—it studies them. Foster a culture that rewards learning over ego and questions over quick wins.
- **Innovation = Liberty in Motion**
  Steve Jobs proved that bold ideas thrive where freedom and discipline meet. Innovation isn't permission—it's a shared commitment to think differently *and* deliver excellence.

# ABOUT THE AUTHOR

**Sharath K. Bhaskaran** is a leadership strategist, writer, and advocate for liberty-centred governance in an interconnected world. With a background spanning organizational leadership, cross-cultural collaboration, and civic engagement, Sharath brings a unique blend of principled thought and practical wisdom to the challenges of modern leadership.

He is the **founder of *Liberty Quill***, a news aggregation platform that distils global insights through a lens of individual freedom and voluntary cooperation. Sharath's work bridge's classical liberal philosophy with the realities of today's diverse workplaces, offering leaders a roadmap rooted in mutual respect, transparency, and empowerment.

Drawing inspiration from visionaries like Gandhi, Douglass, Yunus, and Jefferson, Sharath believes that the best leadership doesn't demand—it invites. It doesn't conform—it inspires. And above all, it multiplies liberty for those it serves.

When he's not writing or advising mission-driven teams, you can find him exploring cultural philosophy, studying decentralized systems, or connecting with communities across continents who are building better futures—one voluntary act at a time.